STORIES & SONGS
OF SIMPLE LIVING

STORIES & SONGS
OF SIMPLE LIVING

Edited by Jym Kruse

ALTERNATIVES FOR SIMPLE LIVING
Sioux City, Iowa

Publisher's Cataloging-in-Publication Data
Kruse, Jym, 1948-
   Stories & Songs of Simple Living
   22.7 cm. 80 pages
   ISBN 0-914966-10-3

1. Kruse, Jym. Stories & Songs of Simple Living. 2. Simplicity - Fiction. 3. Short Stories - Fiction. 4. Storytelling - Fiction.
I. Kruse, Jym, 1948-. II. Title
LC PN   Library of Congress Catalog Card Number: 97-74265
DDC 813/.54

5 4 3 2 1
Printed in the United States of America

Published by Alternatives for Simple Living
PO Box 2857
Sioux City, IA 51106

Alternatives for Simple Living
800-821-6153
www.SimpleLiving.org
109 Gaul Dr., PO Box 340
Sergeant Bluff, IA 51054

For Jan, Brendan and Derek who have lived the story with me.

ACKNOWLEDGEMENTS

We are grateful to the following artists for permission to reprint copyrighted material:

Bill Harley for "Dad Threw the TV Out the Window," © 1988 Bill Harley.

Gayle Ross for her retelling of "The First Fire," © 1986 Gayle Ross.

Dan Keding for "The Tear," © 1995 Dan Keding.

Jym Kruse for "Ninety-Five and Counting," © 1997 Jym Kruse.

Len Cabral for "It's How You Say It," © 1996 Story Sound Productions.

Tom and Chris Kastle for "Song for the Whales," © 1993 Privateer Publishing/Sextant Music.

Michael Cotter for "The Bronco," © 1992 Michael Cotter.

Susan Klein for an excerpt from *The Spirit of the River*, © 1986 Susan Klein.

Joyce Johnson Rouse for "Enough Is as Good as a Feast," © 1994 Rouse House Productions.

Also, thank you to Peter Iversen for the musical transcriptions.

Funded in part by a grant from a friend of storytelling.

Printed on recycled paper.

CONTENTS

FOREWORD

These inspiring stories and songs exemplify the five life principles of Voluntary Simplicity. They are not a manual on "how to" live more simply. Dozens of fine books are available to tell us the reasons to live more simply and "how to" do it. These stories and songs *revel* in it.

The introduction to each piece refers to the life principle which it most directly communicates. Some items touch on several life principles. The five are:

Do Justice
Nurture People
Learn from the World Community
Cherish the Natural Order
Nonconform Freely

For more insight into these principles, read Doris Janzen Longacre's classic work, *Living More with Less*.

The voices of these stories and songs are quite different from each other. Some stories are "moral tales"; some are life experiences. Some are funny; some are quite serious.

Your comments on this collection are welcome.

– Gerald Iversen, National Coordinator, Alternatives

ABOUT ALTERNATIVES

Alternatives for Simple Living – or simply "Alternatives" – is a non-profit organization whose mission is to "equip people of faith to challenge consumerism, live justly, and celebrate responsibly." Started as a protest against the commercialization of Christmas, it encourages celebrations year-round that reflect conscientious ways of living. Throughout its 25-year history, Alternatives has helped lead the movement to live more simply and faithfully. The many staff members and volunteers of Alternatives have developed a wide variety of resources, organized an annual Christmas Campaign, held the Best and Worst Christmas Gift Contest, led numerous workshops, and reached countless people with the message of simple, responsible living. Alternatives emphasizes relationships and traditions over things, hoping to avoid stress and debt, and promoting alternative giving – helping the truly needy instead of spending so much on ourselves.

Alternatives published six editions of the *Alternate Celebrations Catalog* between 1973 and 1987, the final one entitled *To Celebrate: Reshaping Holidays and Rites of Passage.* The new *Treasury of Celebrations* is drawn largely from those six catalogs.

Over the years Alternatives also produced a quarterly magazine and three videos. The most recent video, *Break Forth into Joy!: Beyond a Consumer Lifestyle,* won a

Gold Medal at the Houston International Film Festival.

Alternatives' most widely read resource is *Whose Birthday Is It, Anyway?* This inexpensive, annual booklet for families and small groups, published since 1988, is now available in some 25 different versions for various denominations. All new each year, it contains a daily Advent calendar, reflections on the weekly Bible readings for Advent and Christmas, activities and a variety of other articles.

Alternatives' current catalog of resources includes not only material produced by Alternatives but also books and resources from other publishers – all on simple living and related subjects such as hunger, the environment and media literacy. Because Alternatives provides resources for Advent and Christmas, Lent and Easter, weddings and other celebrations (some in Spanish) for adults and children, Alternatives' motto is *Resources for responsible living and celebrating since 1973.*

Alternatives is funded by grants, donations, memberships and sale of resources. One needn't be a member to use our services. Memberships begin at $25 per year and have numerous benefits.

Contact Alternatives at:

3617 ˘ ¹ ˡ · · · · · ˉ · ˘ oux City,
L   **Alternatives for Simple Living**   orgia)
          800-821-6153
(712   www.SimpleLiving.org   12) 274-1402
E-m   109 Gaul Dr., PO Box 340
Visi   Sergeant Bluff, IA 51054   /AltSimLiv/
     simple.html/

INTRODUCTION

Stories, whether traveling by spoken word or hitching a ride on the melody of a song, have a power which our culture had almost forgotten until quite recently. We always knew we liked a good story, but our busy schedules and the lure of more recent forms of entertainment allowed us to relegate them to a childhood bedtime ritual or a very occasional diversion. Fortunately, a movement has been emerging over the past quarter century which has re-opened our ears to the rich gifts which stories have to offer us. The stories and songs in this edition are of course restricted to ink and paper. Without the printed word to preserve them, many of the stories of even the not-too-distant past would have been lost forever. While the companion audio version of *Stories & Songs of Simple Living* allows one to also hear the oral cadence of the performers, in both forms the stories move our spirits and touch the deeper regions of our memories.

When I approached the storytelling and folk music communities with requests for contributions to an anthology that would feature the widest reaches of living more simply, I had hoped that there would be a positive response. I could not have anticipated how quickly and enthusiastically the project would be embraced. The artists represented here are among the most loved and cherished in their respective communities, and the diversity of their styles adds a rich texture to the canvas of their work.

The focus of this volume is particularly suited to the world of story. To live life more simply has an attractive ring to it, but the stories and songs in this collection demonstrate the much broader implications of simple living. We choose to live more simply not as an end in itself but as a catalyst that enables even more to emerge.

The five life principles that have become foundations for the movement to live more simply illustrate that broader manifestation: do justice, nurture people, learn from the world community, cherish the natural order and nonconform freely. It is difficult to strive for economic justice when our own creature comforts are the only measure of our self-worth. It is even more difficult to nurture the lives of others when the objects we desire take precedence over our relationships. In opening our awareness to lessons within the world community and in noticing that the natural order suffers when the complexities of our lives only consume and never renew, we are sometimes called to act in ways that are alien to the mainstream of our culture – to be productively nonconforming.

All of the pieces offered here address one or more of these issues as they widen our perceptions and call us to a renewed appreciation of the simplest of gifts. Often the reader will find new connections which neither the author nor the editor had anticipated. I hope some of those surprises are also a part of your journey through these stories and songs. May they gently get your attention and then firmly plant the seeds of possibilities you may have long ago forgotten.

– Jym Kruse

ONE

Dad Threw the TV Out the Window

■ **Bill Harley**

Photo by Susan Wilson

Bill Harley

When I hear Bill Harley's voice on my radio (familiar to many people since Bill is a regular commentator on National Public Radio's *All Things Considered*), I remember the powerful effect he had on the audience where I first saw him perform at the National Storytelling Festival. Few artists are able to appeal simultaneously to both children and adults, but Bill has been doing just that as he has shared his unique blend of story and music in thousands of performances over the past decade. He tours nationally to festivals, schools and conferences and has also been featured at the International Children's Festival.

Described by *Entertainment Weekly* as "the Mark Twain of children's music," Harley is especially known for the insight and humor he brings to his observations about growing up and parenting. With a directness and honesty that reveals the details of daily life, he mixes a refreshing dose of fantasy with a healthy breath of reality.

Every one of Bill's ten recordings has won a national award, including five gold awards from the Parent's Choice Foundation. He has also written and narrated award winning film strips and radio dramas and is the author of two children's books.

When a friend of Bill Harley, with a significant temper, got frustrated at his teenage son for not listening, Harley explained that his friend threw the TV out the window. "When he told me what he'd done, I said, 'That's the name of a song!' It sat around for two years waiting to be written; and while the first two verses came easily, it was the last verse that required another six verses. Trying to avoid preachiness, I wrote four last verses before I figured it out. It is the adults, after all, that model behavior for the kids. We watch very little television at our house. We're too busy!"

With "Dad Threw the TV Out the Window," we glimpse not only an image of risking unexpected behavior (nonconforming freely) in the name of our deepest concerns but also a vision of what happens when we allow our time together to be nurturing rather than debilitating.

Dad Threw the TV Out the Window

by Bill Harley

It was in the morn-ing, a sun-ny Sat-ur-day
I turned on the T - V and on the couch I lay I
watched my favor - ite pro - gram and an -
oth - er two or three When my Dad came in the room and
said these words to me "Son, turn off the T - V, there's
lots of things to do Your
bed's not made, the chores aren't done, the
sun is shin-ing too" I said "Dad, I'm bu - sy, I've

got to watch this show" I

guess I should have listen - ed, but

how was I to know? Cause

then he walked a - cross the room and

then he pulled the plug He

lift - ed up the tel - e - vi - sion and

skipped a - cross the rug He open - ed up the win - dow and

then I screamed "Dad, no!" He gave the thing a heave and I

watched the T - V go, oh_____

STORIES & SONGS OF SIMPLE LIVING

CHORUS

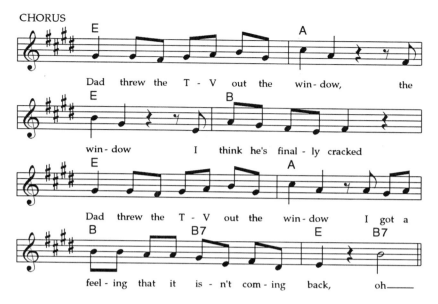

Dad threw the T - V out the win-dow, the
win-dow I think he's final - ly cracked
Dad threw the T - V out the win-dow I got a
feel - ing that it is - n't com - ing back, oh____

II.
When I heard it go,
when I heard it crash
I knew things at our house
would soon be changing fast
My dad looked out the window
and mumbled "My oh my"
My brother looked out too
and said "I'm gonna die"
And that night after dinner
when we went to watch the set
All we found was nothing
I said "How could I forget"
My brother lay down on the floor
and moaned "What will I do?"
But then he told a joke,
and I told two or three
And the one about the elephants
made dad fall on his knees
And mom did her impression
of a duck that couldn't fly
That would have made you
wet your pants
and maybe even cry, all because   CHORUS

Dad Threw the TV Out the Window   5

III.
Life without the TV
wasn't what I feared
I didn't really miss it though
some friends thought I was weird
I didn't miss commercials
and all the blood and guts
And all the stupid shows my brother
watched that drove me nuts
But then one sunny Saturday
my dad could not be found
I looked high and low when
from his room I heard a sound
I ran into his room to see what it could be
I found my father hiding there
watching a TV
I said "Oh, Dad, now really,
you ought to be ashamed"
"I just wanted to watch the game"
I picked up the TV
and waltzed across the room
I gave the thing a heave
and I waited for the boom   CHORUS (I threw the TV)

TWO

The First Fire

■ Retold by **Gayle Ross**

Gayle Ross

"Mesmerizing" is the word often used to describe Gayle's voice, but it is much more than that. Sharply crafted phrases are tempered with a gentle warmth whether she is sharing a personal moment or an ancient story of her people. She is an enrolled member of the Cherokee Nation of Oklahoma and a direct descendant of John Ross, Principal Chief of the Cherokees during the Trail of Tears.

For the past 18 years Gayle has been sharing the stories of the Cherokee people at schools, libraries, colleges and festivals throughout the United States, Canada and Europe. She has two tapes and five books in print and has been named a 1997 Circle of Excellence Award Winner by the National Storytelling Association. Her most recent performances include A Celebration of Books with Tony Hillerman and Maya Angelou; the Cultural Olympiad in Atlanta, Georgia, in conjunction with the Olympics; and A Taste of Tennessee, a Gala at the Vice-President's Mansion. Gayle lives with her husband and two children in Fredricksburg, Texas.

When we reorder our priorities, we also start to notice that the rules about who gets our respect and admiration begin to change as well. For people to be nurtured, our questionable expectations of who constitutes the valuable members of our society must be challenged. When bigger is better and power is our only measure of success, we sometimes conclude that a person's value ought be measured in this same way.

"The First Fire," part of a much longer creation myth, suggests another view. Gayle explains that the story "was traditionally told as a part of the Green Corn Ceremony, the Cherokee time of annual renewal. The telling of the creation story at this time insured that the world of the ancient Cherokee was created anew and would continue. The story teaches an important lesson about the respect which must be given not only to the large and powerful but also to the small and gentle."

•　　•　　•

T his is what the old people told me when I was a
child. In the very beginning days of the world,
the earth was nothing but water – a great
sea – an ocean that stretched from end to end. All of the
people and the animals lived on a great cloud that floated
in the sky vault up above. But it was crowded, and they
were wanting more room. So at last Beaver's grandchild,
the water beetle, offered to go down and see what lay
beneath the water. Now he flew down and landed on the
surface and floated for awhile, resting. Then he dove all the
way to the bottom of the sea and brought back to the
surface the tiniest little handful of mud. He set that mud
floating on the surface of the water, and it grew and
stretched and spread until it became this land floating on
the surface of the sea. But it was still soft and wet, and
there was no place to walk. So the water beetle returned to
the cloud. As time went by, one by one, all of the birds flew
down to see if the land was dry, but it was always too soft
and wet to walk upon.

Finally the great buzzard flew down, and as he flew
across the land and saw that it was still soft and wet, he
grew impatient. When he reached Cherokee country, he
began to fly very close to the land pushing the air on the
land with his great wings, but he flew too close to the
ground. His wings struck the earth, and there was a valley.
Where they lifted up, the tall mountains grew. He kept on
in this way, but the people were afraid that all of the world
would be mountains. So they called him back, but the
Cherokee country is full of mountains to this day.

Now the land was dry. The people and the animals
came down from the sky vault to live, but it was dark. So

the conjurers hung the sun in the sky and set it on a track that moved every day across the land from the east to the west, but they set the sun only a hand's breadth up in the sky. It was too close. It scorched the ground and killed the people. So they moved it up another hand's breadth, but still it was too close to the earth. And another, and another, until finally the conjurers had placed the sun seven hand's breadths into the sky, just beneath the sky vault. And that was right, and the sun traveled its path from east to west every day.

Yet when the sun had left the sky, it was still dark and cold, for the people had no fire. The Thunder Beings, seeing the plight of the people, decided that they would send fire; but fire, with its power to create and its power to destroy, is not a gift to be given lightly. It must be earned. So the Thunderers sent their lightning to strike a hollow tree in the middle of a great lake. The fire burned in that tree, and the people knew it was there for they could see the smoke rising.

Now all of the people and the animals gathered on the shore of the lake, and a great council was held to decide who had the right to bring the fire back from the island. Everyone wanted to be remembered as the fire-bringer, so everyone was eager to try. Finally the great raven was chosen to go. He had no trouble reaching the island; he flew across. But carelessly, as the raven will do, he landed right on the top of the tree; and while he was wondering what to do next, a great blast of hot air came from that tree and burned his feathers black. He was frightened, and he returned without the fire.

Next the little screech owl was chosen to go. He too flew across to the island and landed on the top of the tree, but the smoke and hot air burned his eyes until he could hardly see. He too flew back without the fire. It was a long time before he could see well, and his eyes are red to this day.

Stories & Songs of Simple Living

Next the hooting owl and the great horned owl were chosen to go for they are the wisest of all creatures. Surely they could bring the fire. They flew across to the island and landed on top of the tree, but now the fire was burning so brightly that smoke and ash were floating up from the tree. It burned two, big white circles around the owls' eyes, and scared them so badly that they flew home without the fire. To this day, they keep those great white rings.

No more of the birds wanted to try, so the great bear was chosen to go for he is the bravest and strongest of the animals. Surely he could bring the fire. Now the bear swam across to the island, and when he came to the tree, he climbed into a hole at the base of the hollow tree and found himself on a bed of coals causing him to hunch over and cough. By the time he could make his way out, he was burned black from nose to feet. To this day the bear in those mountains is black. He walks hunched over as though he's still trying to get his breath. He too returned without the fire.

Next the little racer snake was chosen to go for he is one of the swiftest of all creatures. He swam across the water and reached the island. He too went in through that hole at the base of the tree and found himself on that bed of coals. He began twisting and turning and darting and dodging trying to find his way back out. When he came out he was burned black. To this day that little snake, if he is cornered or confused, will begin twisting and turning and dodging in and out as though he is still trying to escape from that tight place.

Now all of the animals fell silent. The wisest, the swiftest, the strongest and the bravest had tried and failed.

Then one, tiny little voice spoke up. It was the little water spider, the little one that dances across the top of the water, asking permission to go. Everyone laughed. If all these great creatures had tried and failed, how could one so tiny succeed? But she pleaded and begged, and at last it was agreed that she should try. She had no trouble reaching the island; she danced across singing. And when she reached the tree, she sat down outside and began singing her power song and spinning her web thread. She spun that thread and spun it and very carefully fashioned her thread until it was a little bowl. She tied that bowl on her back, and reaching inside she took the tiniest little coal of fire and set it in the bowl on her back. Still singing, she danced her way back across the water.

From that little coal of fire were all seven of the sacred fires of the Cherokee lit, and to this day that little water spider keeps that mark on her back, the little round mark of the bowl that she carried. It's there as her badge of honor so that she is remembered as the fire-bringer.

It is to remind us that the gift of heat and light, the power to create and the power to destroy, the gift of fire, was brought to the people not by the biggest or strongest or bravest or wisest or swiftest of all creatures, but by the smallest and meekest of animals.

■

THREE

The Tear

■ Dan Keding

Dan Keding

My first encounter with Dan Keding was at a ghost story concert at the Illinois Storytelling Festival. My oldest son still remembers the sleepless night which followed Dan's particularly effective performance. But Dan tells about much more than ghosts and goblins. He tells of dragons and giants, heroes and heroines, and stories from his boyhood on Chicago's South Side. Dan is also a well respected ballad singer who accompanies himself on guitar, banjo, and spoons. His performances have been called a window into the lore of generations past, creating a path that leads to new insights into the human experience.

His workshops, seminars and performances take him to schools, libraries and festivals around the world. He has been featured at the National Storytelling Festival in Jonesborough, Tennessee; the Sidmouth International Folk Arts Festival, England; and the Towersey Village Festival, England.

Dan's cassette, *Stories from the Other Side*, was recently included in the American Library Association's publication *The Best of the Best for Children*. He is also a recipient of the Distinguished Service Award from the Sun Foundation for Arts and Environmental Sciences.

Fear is a powerful force. While it can help us avoid threatening situations, it can also paralyze us into inaction and make our lives less meaningful. The commitment to a simpler life-style can be laden with fear and uncertainty, but lurking in the shadows of the unknown may be a surprisingly pleasant encounter. Nurturing people is never risk-free, but the rewards are truly enormous.

Dan Keding reflects, "Every day we face fears that are unfounded. We are afraid of failure though failure often brings enlightenment. We are afraid of strangers who after a first meeting become lifelong friends. 'The Tear' is about that fear, about overcoming it and facing the joy that accompanies every new day of our lives."

■　　　■　　　■

Once there was a boy who lived in the foothills of a great mountain range. His job was to take the sheep each day up into the high valleys to graze. His task wasn't hard because his dog did almost all of the work. She herded the sheep, guarded them as they grazed, and brought them back to him at the end of the day. The boy usually found a shady spot where he could sit and play his tambouritza. He loved the old songs that his grandparents would sing and play each night. While the sheep fed, he would sit and play each song over and over again until he knew it by heart.

One day he and his dog took the sheep deeper into the hills than ever before. There they found a hidden valley with long, lush grass. When the sheep saw the grass, they ran into the valley with the dog at their heels. The boy explored the gray hills around him and soon found a rocky cliff. Against the face of the cliff there was a cave so dark that he could only see a few feet into it. At the mouth of the cave there was a big rock, and there he sat down to play his songs. He played for an hour. He played for two. And then he got hungry. He put down his instrument and reached for his lunch. That's when he heard a low and rumbling voice coming from behind him.

"Don't stop playing." The boy looked around, reached for his tambouritza, and was going to run when the voice said, "Please." So the boy played.

After the boy had finished, the voice in the cave told him a story. Then the boy played again, and the voice told him another story. And so it went, all day, story for song, song for story. At the end of the day the boy was filled with wonder. The voice in the cave asked, "Will you come again?" And the boy said, "Yes, tomorrow."

Every day the boy returned to the cave. And every day he heard more stories: stories of knights in battle, stories of

---

adventure, stories of romance, stories of great humor and great sadness, stories of promises kept and promises broken.

One day the boy stayed later than usual. As the sun dropped low over the valley, the voice in the cave grew sad and began to tell its own story, one of loneliness and fear. As the boy listened, he understood that the storyteller was the last of its kind.

Soon the rays of the evening sun began to reach deeper and deeper into the dark cave. As the boy watched, he saw the light glint off the razor-like talons and climb up the powerful legs. Then it reached a huge body that was covered with scales and stretched deep into the darkness. Finally the light followed a long serpent-like neck that arched to hold a great head. Wreathed in smoke and framed by curving horns, the head swayed as the creature spoke. The boy was looking at a dragon.

As he stared at this amazing sight, the boy saw one tear fall from the dragon's eye. Stepping forward, the boy reached out and touched a leathery wing. Suddenly, the great golden eyes of the dragon flew open.

"Aren't you afraid of me?" he roared.

The boy laughed. "No."

"I could rip you apart with my claws."

The boy smiled.

"I could reduce you to a pile of ashes with a single breath."

The boy looked deep into the dragon's eyes. "I can't be afraid of you," he said. "I know your story."

The dragon stared deep into the boy's eyes and nodded. "Will you come tomorrow?"

"Yes."

Every day for many days the boy came back to listen to the dragon's tales and share the songs of his village. One day, as the sun began to set, the boy picked up his tambouritza and turned to face the dragon. "Why do you stay here alone? You could live in the village. My people would love your stories."

The dragon laughed. "Your people and my people have been at war for a thousand years. If I came to your village, the men would all reach for their swords and spears, and there would be a great battle. Many would die, maybe even I."

As the dragon spoke, the boy realized that the dragon's words were true. He made himself a promise to find a way to help his friend.

That night he listened to his grandparents sing and play. When the music stopped, his grandmother said, "Isn't it sad that no one comes to visit our village any more? They all go to the village by the river. And we have such good singers, don't you think?" Hearing his grandmother's words, the boy had an idea. Without waiting for even a minute, he ran to the mayor's house and pounded on the door. The mayor answered the door with a gruff, "What are you doing here at this time of night?"

"Is it true that people have stopped visiting our village?"

"Yes, everyone has forgotten us. Why do you ask?"

"I know someone who could bring the people back – a storyteller – a truly great storyteller."

The mayor smiled. "A storyteller. Yes, everyone likes a good story! I'll go and meet this teller tomorrow and invite him to our village."

Quickly the boy answered, "No. That will never do. You see, he is very shy. He lives in a cave. You will scare him."

"A shy storyteller? I've never heard of such a thing. How am I going to meet him?"

"Well, maybe if you were blindfolded, you wouldn't scare him."

"Blindfolded?!"

"Yes. I'll take you and the village elders to meet him. My dog and I will lead you there."

The next morning, the boy and his dog led the mayor and the village elders up the hillside to the hidden valley. Before they reached the top of the last hill, the mayor and all the elders pulled their blindfolds up and tied them fast. Holding hands, they followed the boy. When they reached the mouth of the cave, they sat in a circle on the ground. The dragon slowly stepped out into the light and began to tell his stories. He told them stories of adventure that stirred their blood, stories of romance that warmed their hearts, funny stories that had them rolling in the grass, and sad stories that made them cry through their blindfolds. Finally, he told them his own story of loneliness. As he spoke, one great tear rolled down his face and landed on the mayor's hand.

Slowly the mayor lifted his blindfold, looked down at the tear and then looked up. With one hand he reached out and touched the dragon. With the other hand he touched the woman next to him. She took off her blindfold and reached out. Around the circle it went until each person was touching the dragon.

The dragon opened his golden eyes and looked at the mayor. The mayor looked back. There he saw an ancient face, creased with untold years of wisdom. "We have come to ask you an important question," he said. "Will you come to our village and be our storyteller?"

In an instant, the dragon replied. "Yes. Yes, I will."

The mayor turned and looked at all the surrounding hills. Then he turned to face the dragon again. "May we ask one favor?" he said with a smile.

"Anything," roared the dragon.

"May we have a ride?"

The mayor, the village elders, the boy, and the dog climbed up onto the dragon's back. He unfolded his huge wings and flew them home. People came from far and near to hear the dragon's stories of promises kept and promises broken.

Years later, when the dragon passed on, he didn't die alone in a cave. He died surrounded by his friends, his great head resting on the lap of a man who had once been a boy and had sung him songs. All the hate and all the fear had disappeared with one tear.

■

FOUR

Ninety-Five and Counting

■ Jym Kruse

Jym Kruse

Since it is my privilege to be the editor of, as well as a contributor to, this volume, I have chosen to include a piece that touches on the personal side of simpler living where it intersects the rhythm of family relationships.

The story connects with the life principles of voluntary simplicity on several levels. Times that our culture sets aside for the giving of gifts often become either a chore or an exercise in self-indulgence. The items we give can become more important than the intended recipient – hardly a formula for the nurturing of people.

Likewise, cherishing the natural order can sometimes be as simple as saying a few words at the right time to encourage an impressionable young mind. When we focus only on our own needs and cater to them uncritically, the implications of our actions reach even beyond the influence they have on other people, as significant as that risk is. The larger realm of those many other creatures with whom we share this planet is also affected. These too become casualties of our desires and our arrogance. Ironically, we sometimes need to look to those who often get ignored to see those truths that are close at hand.

The hope I see embedded within this story is the knowledge that we can draw on our past experiences and learn from our mistakes. The challenge is the knowledge that we do not always choose to do so.

■　　　■　　　■

J eremy didn't even have twenty-four hours left, and he still had no idea what he was going to get his grandfather for his birthday. He kept mentally kicking himself for waiting until the last minute, but he'd been so busy with exams and papers and other necessary-but-less-easy-to-explain activities required of a freshman in college that he hadn't gotten around to finding something. He knew it had to be just the right gift, not only because it was his grandfather's ninety-fifth birthday but because he didn't want to disappoint him. His grandfather meant the world to him.

His little brother suggested he get him a tie. His grandfather hadn't worn a tie in over fifteen years, but his brother often said stupid, irritating things like that. He was used to it. No, this had to be just the right gift. As he walked down that stretch of sidewalk toward the last store he could think of, the hardware store, he was thinking of all the places he'd been so far.

He'd started at the electronics store because it was the one he enjoyed most himself. He knew there wasn't anything there that Grandpa would really need – not because he was old-fashioned. Even at ninety-five, his grandfather was the most modern person he knew. His eyes were still good enough that he could read, and he read about things that Jeremy didn't even study in college. He'd never finished high school, but he loved to talk about the latest discoveries in astronomy and even spoke of Stephen Hawking and wondered if the guy would ever figure out how all those fields of energy worked together.

One time he was talking about inventions and said that the VCR was a much better invention than the TV. It meant that he could watch the few programs that he enjoyed and fast forward through all the commercials that he couldn't stand. It's not that he hated advertising. He'd once

---

Ninety-Five and Counting 21

said, "There are things in this world that a person needs, and it's helpful to know the choices. It's when they try to convince you to buy something that you don't need – don't even want – that's when you've got a problem."

Jeremy had left the electronics place and wandered down the mall to a sporting goods store – also because of his own interest. His grandfather wasn't really the athletic type, but he did like to walk. Countless times Jeremy had been invited to join him on one of his walks in the park. And he knew so much about everything along the way, probably because he paid attention. Often they'd pause to sit on a stump, and it would lead to long conversations and moments that Jeremy would never forget.

One time when he was in fifth grade (while sitting on one of those stumps), he'd asked his grandfather about something a friend had said. They'd been studying the environment, and his friend (doubtless echoing the words he'd heard at home) had said that the world was here to use and it was only crazies who worried about such things. His grandfather got that knowing grin on his face and said, "Sure, there are some silly people out there who overdo things, but I've been around long enough to know that you can't be too careful or care too much. I guess it depends on whether you're planning on having grandchildren."

There were so many memories just like these that had been triggered by Jeremy's fruitless journey that day. The street lights had just come on as he finally arrived at the hardware store. He stood outside the display window wondering why he thought he'd do any better here than at all the other places he had gone and knowing that he was out of choices and out of time. The twilight mingling of street lights and store lights created an interesting combination of reflections on the glass of the store window. As he looked at the merchandise on display inside, it was all a blur to him – his mind still elsewhere in his remembering of all the wonderful times he'd had with his grandfather. Through the blur he caught a glimpse of his own reflection in the glass. In his hazy state of mind, it looked a little like he was inside the store, part of the display, one of the items that had been carefully arranged to catch your attention and draw you in.

The idea didn't form all at once like a lightning bolt – he was too tired for that to happen; but slowly, growing unrelentingly in the depths of his imagination, the idea did make its presence known. He never did focus his eyes well enough to know what was on display behind the glass of that store window. He didn't need to. The idea had finally worked its way to the front of his mind. He knew what to get his grandfather for his birthday, and he still had a lot of work to do.

"In just a little while," was the answer he'd given his mom the last time she checked on him to ask if he was ever planning to go to bed. It was much more than a little while when he finally pushed his chair back from the computer and collapsed in exhaustion to get a few minutes of sleep before he needed to start another day.

The sun was bright in the sky, and a little overly bright in Jeremy's eyes, as they arrived at his grandfather's house. The conversation in the car had followed the usual litany of pronouncements about grandpa's eccentricities and questions about how much longer he'd be able to stay in his own home. Jeremy never liked the word eccentric for his grandfather. His grandfather was simply honest, the kind of honest that cut through the veneer of things that most people prefer to keep covered up. He'd certainly never been a mean person, just uncommonly honest.

When the time came for the ritual of opening the presents, the results were remarkably predictable. His mom and dad had gotten him a lamp that turned on and off by clapping your hands. Grandpa wasn't really feeble enough to require such a thing, but they decided he was old enough that he ought to be. His brother had gotten him a tie – figuring if no one else was going to use his great idea, he would.

The other relatives brought similarly uninspired offerings. Along the way, Grandpa had commented that he was sure he could find a good use for all these things. Jeremy couldn't help but laughing. He had often helped him pack up the gifts from previous such occasions to donate them to people he thought might actually have a use for them.

The time finally came for Jeremy's present. His grandfather started to unwrap it; by then he had lost some of the modest enthusiasm for the process with which he had begun. Lifting the lid off the recycled Avery label box, he saw the carefully hand-bound manuscript.

Jeremy had spent the night putting down on paper a host of memories he had of times with his grandfather and the many lessons and unforgettable aphorisms that had come along with them. Since he knew it was just a beginning, he had titled it simply, *Chapter One*. Leafing through the pages, the impact of the gift was not in doubt even though his grandfather rarely wore his emotions on his sleeve. One's ethnic heritage can leave a powerful residue sometimes.

But there was no mistaking the moisture in his eyes as he nodded his thank you. There was no mistaking the catch in his voice as he said, "If I ever had any doubts, all the effort to make it to ninety-five was definitely worthwhile." And there was no mistaking the smile on Jeremy's face. It felt very good to be able to give a little something back.

■

FIVE

It's How You Say It

■ Len Cabral

Len Cabral

When Len Cabral tells a story, it is a visual experience. From his animated gestures to his dramatically expressive eyes, he engages his audience on every level possible.

Len's strong Cape Verdean ancestry comes alive in his retelling of Cape Verdean, African and Caribbean folktales as well as original stories and other tales from around the world. Using mime, poetry, song, humor and vivid characterization, Len is a popular storyteller at festivals and theaters around the country including the National Storytelling Festival, the Smithsonian's Folklife Festival, the Kennedy Center and the Inaugural Reunion on the Mall Festival.

In addition to authoring children's books for young readers and contributing to several folktale collections, Len also has four audio cassettes one of which has been awarded the Parents' Choice Silver Honor.

A Rhode Island Jefferson Award recipient, Len is cofounder of Spellbinders, Rhode Island's storytelling collective. Len makes his home in Rhode Island with his wife and two teenage daughters.

Taking a risk that can change the world seems out of reach for most of us. Changing the world one little risk at a time often doesn't even catch our attention. Sometimes the most important nonconformist in our world is the one who will take the risk of acting on behalf of what matters when traditional norms would have one look away and ignore the problem. Len takes us to a real street with a real problem and offers us a window into a dilemma we all face from time to time.

"It's How You Say It" offers more than a vision of caring for our world, respecting unlikely people, or even learning the best way to accomplish our goals. It reminds us of the courage required to take even that first step toward making a difference — and why it's worth the risk.

I n the early 70's, I was living in an apartment in Providence right across the street from a building where my brother was working. Every now and then we'd go out to lunch together. One hot August day we had lunch and were driving back to where I lived and he worked. As I was driving up the street, riding down the street on a bicycle that was way, way too small for him was this guy who was huge. He was HUGE! He didn't have a shirt on; all he had on was muscles. He had muscles on top of muscles. He had muscles where most of us don't even have places. He was huge. He was so big he'd make King Kong apologize. That's how big he was. As he was riding down the street, I said to my brother, "Ali, look at the size of this guy!" As he rode by us, he blocked out the sun. We were in the shade. I said, "Wow!"

We continued driving until we came to the community parking lot. I pulled into the parking lot. Right in the middle of the parking lot was a car with its four doors opened and people sitting in the car. The people in the car had just had their lunch. I knew this because everything they didn't eat was on the ground outside their car. There were potato chip bags, soda cans, McDonald's boxes, Dunkin' Donut boxes and banana peels... all this trash.

I said, "No way! They're gonna clean this mess up. I live here, they don't live here. They're cleaning this mess up!"

So I parked the car and my brother and I got out of the car and started walking across the parking lot feeling like a couple of gladiators. All of a sudden I stopped. I noticed, from the corner of my eye, that fella with all the muscles riding that bike back into the parking lot. He got off the bike and gave it back to the little boy whose bike it was. That fella with all the muscles, he walked across the parking lot over to that car and sat down in the driver's seat. It was his car; they were his friends; it was their trash.

Right away I stopped. I had to reevaluate the situation. I said, "Ali, you know, it doesn't look that bad." And it didn't look that bad. "I can always clean it up later, no problem. Come on, let's go."

I thought my brother agreed with me as we walked across the street and stood on the curb on the other side of the street. We watched and we listened as all the doors of that car closed at once, WHOMP. That fella with all the muscles put one hand on the steering wheel and dropped his arm out of the window of the car. His arm was so long it touched the ground. He kick-started the car with a little nudge, his knuckles were dragging on the ground, sparks were coming from his jewelry.

He pulled out of the parking lot into the street. He started to drive by us as I stood with my mouth wide open, when all of a sudden I heard my brother's voice say, "Excuse me. Excuse me." My heart went, "Ping." "Excuse me." The fella driving the car looked at us, reached back and pinched the rear tire of the car and the car stoped. My brother said, "Excuse me, can we have all that stuff over there? You know the banana peels, the soda cans, McDonald's boxes, Dunkin' Donut boxes... can we have all that stuff?"

The guy looked at us, looked at all that trash and then looked back at us. He reached over and grabbed the shift. I was praying he was going to put the car in reverse and not park. He put it in reverse. He released the rear tire of the car. The car rolled back down the street and turned into the parking lot, right into the center of all that trash. He pinched the rear tire and the car stopped. He got out of the car and ordered his friends out of the car. He pointed and they picked, he pointed and they picked. They were as afraid of this guy as I was. They picked up all their trash plus trash that had been there for six weeks. They put it in a big dumpster and got back in the car. The doors all closed, WHOMP. He put one hand on the steering wheel and dropped his other arm out of the window of the car. His arm was so long that it touched the ground. He kick-started the car once again with a nudge. His knuckles were dragging on the ground, sparks coming from his jewelry.

He pulled out of the parking lot into the street and started to drive by us. I'm standing there with my mouth wide open. He looked at us, raised his arm up into the air and gave us a power salute with a big smile on his face as he drove on down the street. I couldn't believe it. My brother nudged me and said, "Len, it's not what you say, it's how you say it." Tact.

■

SIX

Song for the Whales

■ Tom and Chris Kastle

Tom and Chris Kastle

On a beautiful fall day at an outdoor festival near Peoria, Illinois, I shared a stage with Tom and Chris Kastle and for the first time experienced their magnificent gift for putting story into song. Critically acclaimed throughout the United States, in Canada and in Europe, they are known for their good humor as well as their harmonies and varied instrumentation. Several of their original works have been performed and recorded by other artists. As scholars, they have researched the maritime musical heritage of the Great Lakes region and published their findings. As sailors, they have experienced, firsthand, the maritime tradition; Tom is a Coast Guard licensed captain.

They have worked as guest instructors aboard the *Clearwater* and with the Inland Seas Education Association, and as Community Professors in the College of Environmental and Applied Sciences at Governors State University. They also publish the Illinois folk resource, *Common Times*.

While the melody is captivating and continues to play in the heart long after one is done listening to it, the lyrics of "Song for the Whales" are a haunting reminder of how much is at stake in the struggle to care for our world and cherish the natural order.

"This song is loosely based on a true story. Just as the explorers discovered, centuries ago, that the world was not confined to their own 'back yards,' we are coming to know that all life on earth is important and fragile. Hopefully, all of the people of the earth will not delay in learning to work together to restore and preserve all living things great and small, for all living things exist in relation to all other living things. 'It is a song we can all sing together.'"

Song for the Whales

by Tom & Chris Kastle

My father was a whaler and his father before;
I once signed on board back in 1904.
But I vowed to myself, I'd hunt them no more,
When I saw the great humpback break water.

> CHORUS: I sing to the whales as the waters run free,
> As they lunge for the sky and they sound in the sea.
> In their jubilant voices they sing back to me
> Of the joy and the laughter of living.

I first heard their voices so gentle and mild,
And they rang in my ears like the cry of a child.
In the language of ages, they spoke to my soul
Of the bittersweet sadness of parting.   CHORUS

It's a song for the "blue" and a song for the "gray."
It's a song from the past and a song for today.
It's a song on the wind and a song in the spray.
It's a song we can all sing together.   CHORUS TWICE

SEVEN

The Bronco

■ **Michael Cotter**

Michael Cotter

Michael is somewhat of a surprise package. As a third generation Minnesota farmer who farms the flat prairie land that his grandfather first plowed in the 1870's, he looked like a member of the audience waiting for the stories to begin when I first met him one hot summer evening in Illinois. Then he shyly walked to the front of the room and started to speak in his remarkably soft and gentle voice. He began to share a slice of his life with us – true accounts peopled with farmers, town folk, and the wayfarers he has encountered.

After more than ten years of sharing the stories that he has known for most of his life, the style is the same, and that style often evokes magic as listeners and readers begin to hear their own life stories in the memories jogged by Michael's recollections. A lifetime of observing farm animals brings sometimes earthy and sometimes hilarious comparisons between animal nature and human behavior.

As his parenting duties have diminished (and when planting and harvesting permit), Michael now travels around the country sharing his wisdom and his charm.

The "good ol' days" weren't always good, and they certainly weren't always better than what we experience today. Yet there are insights into our humanity and our relationship with the natural order that earlier times may bring to mind if only in contrast to our current mode of thinking.

"The Bronco" is set in a time when people lived more simply – by choice – but when the choices weren't quite as complicated and the pressures to choose something else weren't quite as coercive.

One time in telling this story at a nursing home, an unresponsive resident in a wheel chair, who had given no indication of listening during the story, fluttered his hand just enough to get Michael's attention as he was leaving. Michael got down on his knees in front of him and unexpectedly noticed that his eyes were bright and focused. In a raspy whisper, he said, "One time my dad brought two carloads of broncos, and I helped him." Then his body relaxed.

Michael recalled, "As I drove home I thought of that man, helpless and pitiful; but he knew if he could tell me that he had handled broncos, that I would know that he had once been powerful. He needed to tell me his story, and I had almost missed it."

The act of sharing one's memories – with a child, a new-found friend, or a much larger reading audience – can in itself be a means by which people are nurtured. To do so takes an investment of time and a choice to turn off some of the competition which drives us apart instead of together.

■   ■   ■

Probably the biggest change I saw in my lifetime happened in the period before and after the Second World War. Before the war started, we were a very conserving, frugal society. After the Second World War ended, we became very much of a consuming society. We got electricity on our farm right about then, and our life really changed drastically. There was also quite a bit of money to spend where there hadn't been before.

The story I want to tell you takes place during that Second World War when things were really very different from what they are now. On our farm we had mostly horses as that war started. We had one old tractor with steel wheels, but we had about eighteen or twenty of those big draft horses that weighed two thousand pounds each.

I was the youngest of eight children. I was about twelve years old, and more than anything in the world I dreamed of having a horse to ride. I didn't know enough to ask for an appaloosa or an American saddle bred or a quarter horse. I just wanted a riding horse. Sometimes we would ride those big draft horses, and my feet stuck out. Some of them were really good runners, and some were kind of mean. But they really weren't the most comfortable things, and we weren't supposed to ride them fast. They were for work.

So I begged and begged like kids do. I begged my dad to get me a riding horse, and one day he gave in and said he would. But he never liked to spend a lot of money. That was the common thing to do – you didn't spend a lot of money. So he watched, and one day it was announced in the paper that they were bringing some carloads of broncos in from the West. He thought that might be a good chance for me to get my saddle horse – my riding horse.

It was on a Sunday, and we went to the rail yard. This was before we had those big potbellied semis. The semis were very small and there weren't very many of them, so the livestock was shipped by rail. If you're familiar with Austin, where the new Hormel plant is, that was pasture at that time. Just east of that, where the industrial park is now, that was the rail yard. There were the pens with the railroad tie posts and the high board fences where those old livestock cars came along on the rail and unloaded their livestock, whether it was sheep or cattle or goats. Then they put them in that pasture until it was their time to be slaughtered, and there was always a lot of livestock out in that pasture.

So we went there on this Sunday, and in my mind I dreamed of this beautiful horse. He was going to be black. And he was going to be beautiful. And he was going to have a white star on his forehead. I dreamed and dreamed of this horse and how wonderful he was going to look, and I wasn't prepared for what I saw in that rail yard. These broncos had come out of Nevada where they'd had a prolonged period of drought. In this high pen, huddled in one corner, were these starved horses. They looked like wild animals. Packed into that one corner, they were all watching us, and the whites of their eyes were showing. Their ribs were just skeletons. They had no manes; they were totally eaten off. There was just a scab down their neck. Their tails were eaten off as well; there was just this stump. When they stood, their heads hung except when they put them up with those wild eyes. The people were gathered at the other end, and they were all just sort of starring at each other when we got there.

There were two cowboys. Their skin was about as dark as the wood trim on an old door. They had hats that looked like they'd been on them a long time, and their clothes were dusty. They were sitting on these skinny horses – no manes, no tails, their heads hanging down. When you made your selection, they'd take out a new lariat rope and throw it on the bronco of your choice. Out of that herd of those frightened, skinny broncos would come one plunging and jerking. Then the cowboy handed you the rope, and you got the rope and the horse for $25. That night when I left there, some of those broncos were lying in that dirt. They just would not give in to that rope. To me those cowboys looked like they were old fashioned cowboys, the kind with the hand-rolled cigarette that was fat in the middle and twisted up on the ends. They weren't the real cowboys like we know today – President Reagan or the late John Wayne. These were the old fashioned ones.

Now I'm the youngest of the family. My dad was fifty-five years old when I was born, so he and I had quite an age difference. It's amazing I ever ended up farming because we had a lot of disagreements before I got going; we had a big generation gap. Well, whenever he wanted to intimidate someone, he always called him Shorty. He was a little taller than I am, but that cowboy looked about eight feet tall to me. My dad knew something about these broncos because he'd had them when he was young, and he knew they could be tough and hard to handle, especially the ones that had never had a rope on them. He said to that cowboy, "Hey, Shorty, what'll you take for that horse you're riding?" So for $75 I got the horse the cowboy was riding. He stripped the saddle off him, and I got on his back. Another man that knew my dad, a man who knew something about horses, opened its mouth and after checking his teeth said, "He's just comin' three." He was a young bronco.

I started out with that horse, and when I let him walk, his head hung down. You knew he was broke because he had spur marks from his shoulders clear to his hips, just scabbing over. He had that total arc. He'd had one rough encounter with a cowboy. As long as I owned him if I ever touched my heals to those areas even though they healed up, he would jump like a wild animal.

As I rode him along bareback for home – I was about six miles from home – it wasn't the dream I'd had of that horse; it was a long ways from it. But I had a feel for him. There was something about him I liked even though he didn't hold his head high and he was so skinny. When I got near home, my brother came out to meet us. He wanted to see what kind of a horse I'd bring home, and he laughed when he saw what I had. That made me mad – he's my older brother.

At first my horse wouldn't even eat the alfalfa hay we fed our draft horses. He wouldn't touch it. He wouldn't touch the grain. He'd only eat the weeds along the fence row. Very shortly he did eat that alfalfa hay, and very shortly he did start eating that grain. The energy that hit that horse was almost unbelievable. Pretty soon his head came up and his ears came forward. It wasn't very long until my brother rode him out one day, and the horse came home without him. I didn't even feel bad. I went out looking for him and we both walked home. That horse was coming of age.

Pretty soon that black mane grew in, that deep chestnut coat just shown, those ears came forward, and that neck arched. Those wild eyes were back with that black mane and that black tail. He had a white star on his forehead, and he ran like the very wind. I named him Thunder. And I never had another.

Maybe it was because he'd had too rough a beginning with that cowboy or maybe it was just the way he was. He wasn't a mean horse, but I could never let go of his reins that he didn't run away – except for one time, and that's my story.

A few years had passed. I was probably sixteen or seventeen by then. It was a bitter January like some of the days we had this past January and early February. We had these stock cows. They were Hereford cows – range cows. In the winter they were supposed to be at home on that flat farm where I lived. Then in the spring they would to go up on the hills in the pasture about seven miles away from us and have their calves. But this romance is never quite the way it's supposed to run.

One of these Herefords was going to have a calf on this January day, and one of the characteristics of a Hereford cow is to go off by itself when it has its young. This was before we had snow blowers or even scoops on our tractor, and that cow was missing this one bitter Sunday morning. She was gone. She'd gotten away and gone off by herself. So I took that bronco.

Now a neighbor boy had been dragged to death by a horse about the time I was born, so my dad said there'd never be a saddle on our farm. That was the rule I lived under, so I went all those years riding bareback. That's still the way, if I rode, that I'd be most comfortable – riding bareback.

I started out looking for that cow. On the far corner of our farm, the most remote corner at that time, where there was a slough with long grass and some brush and where Interstate 90 runs now, that's where I found her. The calf had already been born. He was lying in that tall grass. His ears where already frozen, and the snow was just drifting over him. She'd washed him off, and she was standing there with her head over him. As I came upon her, it was like so many things in nature. She had done everything she could, and they were both just waiting very quietly for the inevitable. It looked like a scene from some famous painting.

I came along with that bronco whose reins you couldn't let go of, and I knew there weren't going to be many chances to get that calf out of there. He was freezing to death. I got down, and I was trying to hold that horse and trying to pick up that calf. It wasn't working.

I don't know what it was, maybe it was the desperation in my voice, but I remember saying to that horse, "You've gotta stand." And I let go of his reins and I picked up that calf. If you know what a newborn calf is like, they're like a sixty pound angleworm. They're slippery, and they're kicking and moving.

In my mind I can still see that horse. His ears were pointed and his neck was arched. His nostrils were flared as he snorted. That white ring, that wild look, was back in his eyes. He danced around me, but he didn't run. Somehow I got that calf up on his back. Somehow I got up behind him, and we went home. And the cow followed. And the calf lived. And I never let go of his reins again but what he ran.

■

EIGHT

The Spirit of the River

■ Susan Klein

Susan Klein

Most storytellers are enjoyable to listen to, but when Susan Klein tells a story, it is a truly enthralling experience. With a voice that is as smooth as it is riveting, she plays the role of spellbinder, and we are soon willing participants in the adventure in which she engages us.

Susan makes her home on the Island of Martha's Vineyard in Massachusetts where she was born and raised, but much of her time is spent touring her one-woman shows in theatres, schools and at conferences. She also appears on radio and television and leads highly acclaimed storytelling workshops nationwide and in Europe.

Her repertoire includes selections from folklore and myth, literary stories, audience participation stories for children, rites of passage and love stories for adults of all ages. The autobiographical stories draw on her Martha's Vineyard childhood, her experience as a teacher and her work as an itinerant storyteller in the Alaskan Yup'ik Eskimo villages of the Lower Kuskokwim River Delta.

In addition to appearances at the National Storytelling Festival and serving as Guest Host for Minnesota Public Radio's "Good Evening" show, "Beach Party," one of Susan's original stories from her book, *Through a Ruby Window*, was featured on ABC NEWS NIGHTLINE.

Our world is filled with people who live their lives in ways much different from our own. Many still cling to values which care for the earth and respect other people. Many prize people over possessions. Many live in ways that offer lessons from which each of us could learn.

The Spirit of the River *is a personal journey into a lifestyle both unexpected and transforming – definitely simpler than many of our lives, but profoundly rich in the qualities that make those lives worth living.*

．　　　．　　　．

W hen I first came to the tundra, I was not quite
prepared for what I would find. I had lots of
ideas about going to a place where there
would be many stories and where maybe I would live a
story or two. I was certainly bringing some stories with
me. But I didn't know that when I went to that first village,
that tiny village of only forty-five people, that when I was
delivered there by a truck that traveled on the river, for the
river became the highway when it was frozen, I didn't
know that as I stepped out of that truck and looked at
those fourteen houses – quiet, there was not a sound – it
was so quiet (a good distance away there was someone
sitting there on the ice, fishing, jigging) – I didn't know the
feeling that I would have, which was that I had come
home.

I walked into the village, all of my things sitting out on
the ice. The little man in the truck had driven away, and
there was no one there to greet me. It looked like there was
no one in the village at all. I walked through the village on
the boardwalks though they were iced over. They were all
connected house to house so that when the thaw came it
would still be easy to get from one place to another. With
all the standing water, it would not have been good were
there nothing to walk upon between the houses. It would
have been very soggy on the small bit of the permafrost
that melted in the good weather.

I walked down the boardwalks past that great, central
pile of driftwood that had been taken out of the river in the
warmer months. I walked between the houses, and still
there was no one stirring. Then suddenly I saw this tiny,
little head peek out. It came out from the back of the

school, and that little head looked at me with very shiny eyes. He looked to be about nine or ten years old. I waved. He waved. I beckoned. He shook his head, "No." I beckoned again. He shook his head, "No." By then we were both smiling, and he came forward.

He said, "Who are you?"

I said, "I'm Susan. I'm the storyteller."

"Where did you come from?"

"I came from Massachusetts, and I'm here to tell stories in the school for the week. Could you take me to the school?"

"Where did you get that hair?"

"My hair? I was born with this hair. It just grows this way." I had great, long locks of very curly hair at the time. They were sticking out all over the place around my hat.

He said, "No! Hair does not grow like that."

I laughed as I said, "Yes, it does grow like that."

He said, "No! Hair is straight and black, not all 'windy' like that."

I said, "No. Here maybe all of the people have straight hair, but where I come from you can have different colors of hair, and sometimes it's not straight. Sometimes it's curly like this."

"No! Hair is black... Where did you get those eyes?"

Laughing again, I said, "The eyes came from the same place that the hair did."

"No! Eyes are not green. Eyes are black like mine."

"Well, I imagine so, but where I come from you can have green eyes or blue eyes and sometimes a combination of the two, or brown eyes or black eyes. And these eyes are green."

"No!"

I said, "Well, is there anything else?"

"Where did you get that, uh... You have a lot of nose."

And then he laughed and laughed, and I laughed and

laughed. And we walked together to the school. That was my introduction to an Eskimo child who was one of the most dear things. He had a way of teasing in the world that was delightful. He knew what he knew, and he could always turn it into humor. I found that was generally the rule. There was so much humor to be found here.

So we went into the school. We brought in all of my things from the river, and I began to settle in to this tiny, little school where the teacher had come from a long ways across the country, and when she got there her housing had not been finished – it hadn't been started. So she lived in the school. And every morning at 7:00 there would be faces in mine saying, "Susanaq, wake up. It is time to start the day."

The children would already be there at the school at 7:00 though it didn't start until 9:00. They would come and visit, and oh, how we visited. We talked and listened to one another. It was wonderful. The very first day that I had gotten myself together to tell stories was a Monday. I had known everybody already by the time school started that day. When you have a village of forty-five people and there's a new girl in town, it's an important thing to find out who that new girl is – everyone had come to visit. So on Monday I said to them all as they sat before me, "Do you like stories?" That was greeted with silence.

I said, "Does anyone tell you stories at home?" – Silence.

Finally I said, "Are you all ready to listen to some stories?" – Silence.

I thought to myself, this is really something. What am I going to do with all of these children? They seemed to understand me yesterday when we talked. What's going on?

Finally, Steven, the boy whom I had met outside the school the day before, came up to me. He said, "Susanaq, why are you yelling at us?"

I said, "Oh, I'm sorry. I didn't know that I was yelling?"

He said, "You're talking very loud."

I said, "Well, you're not answering me, and I'm wondering if you heard me. What's wrong?"

"Nothing is wrong."

"Well, I don't understand."

He said, "Try it again."

So I said, "Do you all like stories?" – Silence.

I said, "Steven, why won't anybody answer me?"

He said, "We all answered you."

"I didn't hear anything."

He said, "Watch this." He took his hand. He put it on his forehead so that he pulled up his straight, black hair, and showed me his forehead and his eyebrows.

He said, "Ask me a question again."

I said, "Do you like stories?"

And then I *saw* the answer. As a matter of fact, it was a very loud silence. "Yes," to the Eskimo children was a raise of the eyebrows. Because they all had long, straight hair that hung over their eyebrows, I couldn't see it; nor had anyone told me that that was the situation.

So I learned my first lesson: to always expect the unexpected. And did we laugh! They all sat there and giggled and giggled. With just a few more days in the village, I found that by the time I left, I too was answering with my eyebrows when I was asked a question.

One day while I was there, one of the women of the village, who happened to be the cook in the school, came to talk to me. We had been chatting during the week, and I had been really enjoying her. She was the mother of five of the children in the school, which means that she had a maternal influence over one-third of the school population in that village. Maggie was her name.

Maggie said to me, "I would like you to try my dryfish."

Now I had seen the dryfish hanging on the racks outside of the houses. The way that the fish hung was ingenious to me. The heads had been chopped off, and then with their *ulugs*, the fan-shaped blade that the Eskimos use, they had sliced down the sides of the backbone and the backbone was removed. There were actually two fillets of fish, but they were still connected by the tail. Then using the blade to go through the fish but not through the skin, it was scored in a number of ways so that the fish spread out a bit and got more surface area to the sun in the summer time when it was drying out on those racks. It hung by the tail.

Because it was salmon, it was a beautiful color of orange. You would see those great, wide splashes of orange across the little village. They were wonderful to see because the colors in the tundra in the winter are mostly gray and white. Since there are no trees, the houses stand tall on this scape line and there are these bands of orange that add wonderful color in an otherwise rather dim existence.

So when she said she wanted me to try her dryfish, I was excited. I'd heard about dryfish when I was in the city on the way to this village, but I was not prepared for what happened.

The next day Maggie brought me a fold of aluminum foil and handed it to me. She said, "My family loves my dryfish, I hope you like it too." I opened it up, and I was not prepared for what I saw. There, where I expected to see this beautiful bright orange fish, I saw nothing but green and black, very fuzzy mold. I thought, "Oh, no! How am I going to eat this?" I certainly did not want to be offensive, and I thought, "Well, if this is the way it's eaten, then this is the way it's eaten."

I got myself ready and picked up the piece of fish. I was wondering how I was going to be able to eat this knowing that it was going to be very funny for me to express the truth if I really hated it, but I do my best to always tell the truth. So I took a great big chunk of this fish in my mouth. I pulled and pulled until it came off of the skin, and I chewed.

You might guess that green and black fuzzy mold tastes exactly the way you think it might – terrible! But underneath, the flavor of the dried salmon began to overpower the taste of the mold. When that salmon flavor came through, it was delicious. In the meantime, I felt like I had all these little sweaters on my teeth, and it felt so weird inside my mouth. I finally swallowed it, and I was getting myself ready to tell Maggie how good the fish tasted (and try to ask her about the mold) when I looked up. Her otherwise rather small eyes were gigantic.

She looked at me and said, "Susanaq, you eat the mold?!"

I said, "Maggie, don't you?"

She said, "No! I would not eat that mold." She took a piece of wet paper towel and wiped off the mold on the other piece of fish she had until all of it was gone. That beautiful orange color was shining through, and then she ate her piece of fish that way.

I said, "Why didn't you tell me?"

She said, "You are a girl from far away. I don't know what you eat."

So I got another lesson in telling the truth. If I had said something beforehand, she definitely would have let me know that eating the mold was not part of the plan; but because I didn't say anything, there I was, stuck with it. And did we laugh after that! Of course the entire village heard about it, and everybody laughed because I had been tricked. And that sense of humor came rolling through again. I loved it.

I loved the fish. So I sat down with her, and we wiped off the mold, and I ate the dryfish and drank the tea, very strong tea. It is a wonderful combination. Then we talked much about her children. We talked about the village and the ways there.

I went out for a walk later that day. The children followed me; I was doing some photography. There was a row of boats. They were bigger than rowboats, square on one end and pointed at the bow. They were all upturned on a rack about two feet above the ground next to a framework that looked like a tiny hut but without walls or ceiling or floor – just the framework. The children explained to me that this was one of the fish camps and that in the springtime, when school got out, the families all gathered themselves up and went off to fish. They fished all the late spring and the summer in order to create enough food for the wintertime to supplement the hunting and the trapping.

One of the boys, Andrew, as we walked by the boats, trailed his fingers along the bottom of the stern of one of the boats. He turned to me and said, "My father built this boat." It had been a long time since I had heard that kind of pride in the voice of a child speaking about something that had been handmade by a parent.

I took pictures of them on the slough. They were grabbing a rope that had been hooked up to one of the houses by the slough. They would run and jump on this rope. There was an old boat that had been abandoned. It was sitting on the shore of the slough. So they could fly on this rope out onto the boat, and they would have a wonderful time. It was almost like swinging on a vine in a jungle with that same kind of freedom of flight but still with some security. They would fly out to the boat, climb down the side of the boat, and then run back up the hill, grab onto this rope again and fly out to the boat once more.

This game went on for quite some time. As I watched them, I was aware of that cycle and that circular motion that all of us seem to put into our patterns when we can: from the rope to the boat to the ground to the rope and back again. The circle of play and that circle of work that we do – for when we're children our work oftentimes is our play and our play is our work. I looked at the other circles. There were the circles the houses made around that great "fire" that was in the middle. It seemed like a fire, but it was actually the firewood that was the community lot for anyone who needed fuel. Everyone had gathered that together when the driftwood had come down the river during the thaw. And I noticed the circle that they created in their lives, that annual circle of gathering and eating and trapping and fishing and hunting.

I noticed the circles, and the circle seemed complete to me.

■

NINE

Enough Is as Good as a Feast

■ Joyce Johnson Rouse

Joyce Johnson Rouse

While her musical style ranges through reggae, dixieland, calypso, pop and folk, the theme of sustainable living is a frequent one in Joyce Rouse's work. She grew up on a farm near Cresco, Iowa, where the music of the Earth touched her at an early age, and she has been singing and writing ever since.

She has been a Nashville songwriter and performer for over ten years, and her song, "Standing on the Shoulders," premiered at the national celebration of the 75th Anniversary of Women's Suffrage in Washington, D.C. She is the creator, writer and performer of the EARTH MAMA music projects in which she combines her music, humor and entertainment gifts with her concern for the Earth.

With "Enough Is as Good as a Feast," we come full circle. In very personal terms, it challenges the forces within our society that would have us long for more things to sustain economic "progress" while making vulnerable the sustainability of the Earth itself.

Joyce says that in the process of creating her music, she often finds it to be a spiritual experience and that it was particularly true in this case. "In the early months of 1994, I was coming through a very low period of my life, and I believe I wrote this song as an exercise in counting my blessings. The more verses I wrote, the richer I felt!"

Ultimately we must come to the realization that a simpler life-style is not about what we give up or endure "for the cause." Rather, it is about making choices that actually enrich our lives with treasures whose value is measured on a different scale from the trinkets of everyday commerce but whose worth is profound and lasting. On a global scale, those choices determine whether the riches of our planet will be justly available to all or wastefully consumed by a few.

We have been given gifts beyond measure. We have opportunities to cherish those gifts and live well in their bounty. Now we have choices to make. Enough is as good as a feast!

Enough Is as Good as a Feast

by Joyce Johnson Rouse

I've got a tur-tle-neck sweat-er in my fav'-rite shade of blue, and a crack-lin' fire to warm me when a cold front's com-in' through. A win-dow for air con-di-tion-ing and the shade of a map-le tree, I've got e-nough, e-nough, e-nough is as good as a feast. I've got a tat-tered book of po-e-try that's filled with all the greats. Dick-in-son and Ro-bert Frost An-gel-ou and Yates. An old pi-an-o for mu-sic and a

---

song that plays for free, I've got e - nough, e -

nough, e - nough is as good as a feast.

I don't need a man - sion or a

gen - ie to grant me a wish. I be - lieve that

he who knows he has e - nough is

rich. Out back there's a

gar - den that bless - es my spring with peas.

La - ter on in the sum - mer with to -

ma - toes and beans. Sweet Will - iams and

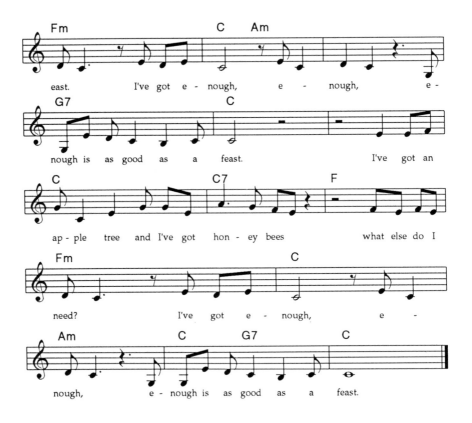

east. I've got e - nough, e - nough, e -

nough is as good as a feast. I've got an

ap - ple tree and I've got hon - ey bees what else do I

need? I've got e - nough, e -

nough, e - nough is as good as a feast.

RESOURCES

The following list of resources is offered for those who are interested in other stories and songs by the artists represented in this collection or more information about Alternative for Simple Living. Information on booking performances is available at the address indicated with each artist.

LEN CABRAL

Story Sound Productions
30 Marcy St
Cranston, RI 02905
(401) 781-0019

Audio
Ananzi Stories, Cassette
It's How You Say It, Cassette
Nho Lobo, Cassette
Stories for the Wee Folk, Cassette

Books
Anansi's Narrow Waist, Addison Wesley Publishers 1994
Len Cabral's Storytelling Book, Neal-Schuman Publisher, Inc. 1997

Michael Cotter

Rt 3 Box 47
Austin, MN 55912
(507) 437-3306

Audio
Amazing Grace, Cassette
Dad's Stories and Farm Memories, Cassette
Minnesota Seasons, Cassette
People of the Earth, Cassette
Stories of the Land, Cassette

Book
Memories: A Collection of Personal Stories by Michael Cotter

Bill Harley

301 Jacob Street
Seekonk, MA 02771
(508) 336-9703

Audio
50 Ways to Fool Your Mother, Round River Records 1986
Already Someplace Warm, Round River Records 1994
Big Big World, A&M Records 1993
Come On Out and Play, Round River Records 1990
Cool in School: Tales From 6th Grade, Round River Records 1987
Coyote, Round River Records 1987
Dinosaurs Never Say Please, A&M Records 1987
From the Back of the Bus: Completely True Stories by Bill Harley,
    Round River Records 1995
Grownups are Strange, Round River Records 1990
I'm Gonna Let It Shine: A Gathering of Voices for Freedom, Round
    River Records 1990
Lunchroom Tales: A Natural History of the Cafetorium, 1996
Monsters in the Bathroom, Round River Records 1984
Peter Alsop & Bill Harley: In the Hospital, Moose School Records 1989
*Sitting on My Hands: A Collection of Commentaries as Aired on
    National Public Radio's All Things Considered*, Round River
    Records 1995
Wacka Wacka Woo and Other Stuff, Round River Records 1995
You're in Trouble, A&M Records 1988

Video
Who Made This Mess?, A&M Records 1992

Books
Carna and the Boots of Seven Strides, Riverbank Press 1994
Nothing Happened, Tricycle Press 1995
Sarah's Story, Tricycle Press 1996
Sitting Down to Eat, August House Publishers 1996
You're in Trouble, August House Publishers 1997

TOM AND CHRIS KASTLE
Sextant Music, Ltd.
6342 W Belmont
Chicago, IL 60634
(773) 714-0328

Audio
Burnham Harbor, CD and Cassette
Earthways, Waterways, CD and Cassette
Strike the Bell, CD and Cassette
That Time of Year: Songs and Stories of Christmas, CD and
    Cassette (with Dan Keding)
See the Sea: Songs for Younger Sailors, Cassette

Video
The Mermaid and Other Sea Songs

DAN KEDING
PO Box 1701
Springfield, IL 62705
(217) 787-1448

Audio
Dragons, Giants, and the Devil's Hide, Cassette
Homework: Songs and Stories for Kids, Cassette
MacPherson's Lament, Cassette
Promises Kept, Promises Broken, Cassette
Rudy and the Roller Skate, Cassette
South Side Stories, Cassette
Stories from the Other Side, Cassette

That Time of the Year, Cassette

Video
The Large Mouth Frog

SUSAN KLEIN
Box 214
Oak Bluffs, MA 02557
(508) 693-4140

Audio
Aphrodite's Nosegay, Cassette
Old Standbys, Cassette
Spirit of the River, Cassette
Through a Ruby Window, Cassette
Willie the Bug Man, Cassette
Wisdom's Tribute, Cassette

Books
And Now, Would You Please Welcome…, edited by Carol Birch &
   Melissa Heckler
Through a Ruby Window, August House

JYM KRUSE
2619 Pawnee Meadows Rd
Fremont, NE 68025
(402) 721-1253

Audio
Stories from the Four Corners of the World, Cassette
Telling the Truth: Stories to Bring Us Together, Cassette
Well Traveled Seeds, Cassette

GAYLE ROSS
Hodges & Hodges Performing Arts
PO Box 158
Johnson City, TX 78636
(210) 868-4337

Audio
To This Day, Cassette

How Rabbit Tricked Otter, Cassette (Parabola Storytime Series)

Books
How Rabbit Tricked Otter, Harper Collins
The Girl Who Married the Moon, Bridgewater Books (with
    Joseph Bruchac)
How Turtle's Back Was Cracked, Dial Books for Young Readers

JOYCE JOHNSON ROUSE

Rouse House Productions
PO Box 1284
Brentwood, TN 37024
(615) 370-4032
http://www.songnet.com/earthmama/

Audio
Love Large, CD
Earth Mama, Cassette
Every Day is Earth Day, Cassette
Around the World with Earth Mama, CD (13 songs from *Earth
    Mama* and *Every Day is Earth Day*)

ALTERNATIVES FOR SIMPLE LIVING

PO Box 2857, Sioux City, IA 51106
Call 800-821-6153 anytime for a free copy of Alternatives'
current Resource Guide (catalog). Or visit on-line:
http://members.aol.com/AltSimLiv/simple.html/

• *Seasonal* Materials

Whose Birthday Is It, Anyway? Christmas booklet.
    Alternatives provides people with ideas to celebrate responsibly in
this Advent/Christmas Resource. Designed for individuals, families
and small groups, the booklet is all new each year and includes Biblical
reflections, services for special times (such as decorating the home and
food preparation), activities, a touching story, an Advent calendar and
suggestions for remembering those in need. *Whose Birthday Is It,
Anyway?* is available in quantity pricing.
    The Advent/Christmas Calendar in *Whose Birthday Is It, Anyway?*
is also available as a poster, as bulletin inserts and in Spanish.
    Order copies – English/Spanish poster; English bulletin insert. Or
copy it. Pay Alternatives a small royalty. It can be used as a poster, a
flyer or a bulletin insert.

Resources   **61**

Simplify & Celebrate! Embracing the Soul of Christmas
> This large collection shows how to have a More Meaningful, Less Commercial Celebration. The 1997 book includes several sets of meditations on the readings for Advent through Epiphany for personal and group/family reflection, sermon preparation, etc. Each volume of this projected multi-volume series contains ideas, articles, stories and activities for families and church leaders. Simplify & Celebrate! includes over 25 writers – Joan Chittister, Michael Crosby, Mike and Kathe Sherer, Carolyn Hardin Engelhardt, Milo Thornberry, with illustrations by Kathie Klein.
> Northstone (Wood Lake Books), 1997, 192 pp.

Sing Justice! Do Justice! A Collection of New Hymns and Songs
> The five winning entries and some fifty Honorable Mentions from the over 200 entries in the international contest cosponsored by Alternatives and The Hymn Society in the United States and Canada. Texts and music ready for personal or group use.

Leader's Guide to the Unplug the Christmas Machine Workshop
Jo Robinson & Jean Coppock Staehali
> Alternatives has received an exclusive license to reissue this companion to the classic *Unplug the Christmas Machine*. This guide helps leaders create a four hour workshop that helps participants clarify their beliefs and make realistic plans for more joyful, meaningful celebrations. A Participant's Manual is included and can be photocopied. Convenient packet format ready for your three-hole binder.

Unplug The Christmas Machine: A Complete Guide to Putting Love & Joy Back into the Season
Jo Robinson and Jean Coppock Staeheli
> With thoughtful suggestions, creative exercises and answers to often-asked questions, this book helps people create celebrations that give them joy and satisfaction.

Let's Talk About Christmas! Worksheet
> Instead of going on autopilot the day after Thanksgiving, let this worksheet guide you through your Christmas Revival. Talk about what each of you really wants at Christmas, about expectations, about who is going to do what. Anytime will work, but aim for October 1st.

Have Yourself a Merry Little Christmas VIDEO
Explore creative ways to de-commercialize Christmas with this provocative video. Vivid photography, music and interviews help us rethink how we observe this holy day. It is an ideal way to introduce people to the idea of celebrating more simply and meaningfully. VHS, 17 min.

Gifts of Peace Resource Packet
Contains study guides, bulletin insert, giving guide and current calendar for churches and groups.

A Christmas Reader
These old and new stories, well-loved poems and a prayer reflect the true spirit of Christmas. 24 pp.

A Christmas Collection
Remember the real reason we celebrate by singing a carol, reading a Christmas story or listening to actual stories of special gifts. 24 pp.

A Christmas Sampler
Classics and stories from different countries. Greetings in 31 languages. 28 pp.

The Christmas Stories SET
All three collections above for a special price.

Behold That Star: A Christmas Anthology
These stories, poems and carols are meant to "bring to Christmas something other than tinsel and outward show." 368 pp.

40-Day Calendar for Lent
New each year.

Alternatives offers many children's books. Call for a catalog.

- **Year-round materials:**

  The Alternative Wedding Book
  > Create a beautiful Wedding that reflects your values &
  > doesn't cost the earth.
  > Soft cover edition. Description below. Northstone, 1995, 124 pp.

  Wedding Alternatives Packet. A Guide to Planning Out-of-the-
  Ordinary Celebrations
  > When a couple is bombarded by consumer, cultural and
  > family pressures to have the "perfect" wedding, their wedding
  > can become a social event rather than a significant religious and
  > personal celebration. In a three-hole punch format, this packet
  > offers engaged couples, clergy and others involved in planning
  > weddings practical advice and personal stories from people who
  > chose to incorporate their values into their ceremony and
  > celebrations. Included are ideas on vows, location, food, flowers,
  > invitations and much more. Permission to copy parts of the
  > packet is granted with your purchase. Alternatives, 1992.

  Nuestra Boda. Guia Para una celebracion fuera de lo comun
  > Spanish translation of our popular *Wedding Alternatives.* In
  > addition to the information from the English version, *Nuestra*
  > *Boda* includes ideas and personal stories from Hispanics in
  > several countries. Alternatives, 1995.

  Treasury of Celebrations. Create Celebrations That Reflect Your
  Values and Don't Cost the Earth
  Carolyn Pogue, editor
  > *Alternatives' Treasury of Celebrations* channels our desire to
  > celebrate into activities that truly nourish the human spirit,
  > express our solidarity with all the earth's people, and respect the
  > environment. It helps us resist consumer pressures and celebrate
  > in a more spiritually fulfilling, joyful way. If you are not satisfied
  > with consumer-oriented celebrations, this big book of creative
  > ideas is for you.
  > *Treasury* contains life giving ways to celebrate weddings,
  > birthdays, Bar/Bas Mitzvahs, funerals, Christmas, Hanukkah,
  > New Year's Day, Valentine's Day, Purim, Easter, Shavuot,
  > Remembrance/Memorial Day, Hiroshima Day, Halloween,
  > Thanksgiving, graduations, and other holidays and rites of
  > passage.
  > *Treasury* draws material from the six Alternate Celebrations
  > Catalogs published from 1973-87 by Alternatives and adds new
  > ideas as well.
  > *Treasury of Celebrations* has a unique "alternative" approach

to planning celebrations, is values-based, includes anecdotes of
real celebrations, and contains practical planning ideas and
details for activities.
Northstone division of Wood Lake Books, 288 pp., 1996.

To CELEBRATE. *Reshaping Holidays and Rites of Passage*

Encouraging joy, spontaneity, justice and concern for nature,
this sixth edition of the Alternative Celebrations Catalogue is for
people who are not satisfied with the models of celebration
offered by a consumer society. Included are the celebration
experiences of people with widely varying backgrounds and
perspectives. Alternatives, 224 pp., 1987.

Break Forth Into Joy! Beyond a Consumer Life-style

Now in Video and Audio

Winner of the GOLD MEDAL Houston International Film
Festival! *Break Forth Into Joy!* examines our search for fulfillment
and security through material possessions. By sharing feelings,
thoughts and practical ideas from a variety of people, this video
explores consumerism and its effects on people, the Earth and the
human spirit. With a call for change, *Break Forth Into Joy!*
encourages people to nurture their communities and their spirits
by living more responsibly and joyfully.

Following the main 15-minute segment are three additional
10-minute sections that encourage further thought and discus-
sion on freedom and possessions, family and children, and
taking action. Use this video to provoke thought on life-style
issues in your congregation or community. Use it to introduce a
special event, workshop or conference. For more in-depth study,
use the accompanying study guide with a Sunday school class or
small group.
Break Forth into Joy! VHS or Audio Cassette and Study Guide, 45
minutes total, 1994.

Shalom Connections in Personal and Congregational Life
Dieter Hessel, editor

This study guide helps individuals and congregations
examine life-style issues. It offers ideas for responsible living that
reflect peace, justice and simplicity.
Alternatives, 160 pp., 1986.

The Simpler Living Alternatives Calendar for Any Year

The Simpler Living Alternatives Calendar strives to help change
our wasteful habits into Creation-Conserving, Earth friendly
ones. We can start by living the Environmental Tithe – by

---

reducing our consumption by at least 10%." The word "tithe" means "a tenth" or 10%.

This 366 day calendar can be used during ANY year. Start any day... Start TODAY! Time and seasons are circular, continuous. Time does not begin with January and end with December. Jump in ANYWHERE. The calendar includes no days of the week.

This calendar attempts to influence various aspects of our lives. It is designed for people at any level of commitment and ability. Each month has a theme and several related topics as well as time to Contemplate, to Self-evaluate, to Investigate and to Act.

Alternatives' Any-Year Calendar comes as a flip-style Desk Calendar (one day per page) or as Bulletin Inserts. Alternatives provides a complete set of reproducible bulletin insert masters but not preprinted bulletin inserts.

Read each day's thought alone, with the family, in a study circle or small group, or with your faith community. *Use it at home, at the office, as church bulletin blurbs, newsletter fillers, etc.*

The 4x5 inch pages are printed on 100% recycled chlorine free paper (75% post-consumer waste) using soy-based ink. Alternatives, 1997. Quantity pricing available.

Stories & Songs of Simple Living
Jym Kruse, editor

Popular American storytellers and folk singers – men and women from various ethnic backgrounds – tell and sing their own works in this inspiring new book and tape collection *for all ages*. Read the book alone or aloud. Listen to the tape at home or in the car. Or listen and follow along.

Book and tape available separately or as a specially priced set. Also available at a discount with *Sing Justice! Do Justice!*

NATIONAL STORYTELLING ASSOCIATION
PO Box 309
Jonesborough, TN 37659
(423) 753-2171

The best source for information about storytellers, storytelling resources and storytelling events in your area. They also sponsor the National Storytelling Festival each October in Jonesborough, Tennessee.